Tables Of Ancient Literature And History, B.c. 1500-a.d. 200

TABLES OF

ANCIENT LITERATURE

AND HISTORY.

Published by

JAMES MACLEHOSE, GLASGOW.

———

MACMILLAN AND CO., LONDON AND CAMBRIDGE.

London, ... *Hamilton, Adams & Co.*
Edinburgh, ... *Edmonston & Douglas.*
Dublin, ... *W. H. Smith & Son.*

MDCCCLXXVII.

TABLES

OF

ANCIENT LITERATURE

AND HISTORY.

B.C. 1500—A.D. 200.

BY

JOHN NICHOL, LL.D.,

PROFESSOR OF ENGLISH LANGUAGE AND LITERATURE, UNIVERSITY OF GLASGOW.

GLASGOW:

JAMES MACLEHOSE, 61 ST. VINCENT STREET,
Publisher to the University.

1877.

GLASGOW:
Printed at the University Press
BY ROBERT MACLEHOSE, 153 WEST NILE STREET.

EXPLANATORY NOTE.

IN drawing up these Tables of Ancient History and Literature, an attempt has been made to give a synoptical view of the chronological relation of the fortunes and achievements of the nations in whose history and development students are mainly interested.

The following are the general features of the plan which has been adopted :—

1. The *arrangement of the Columns* varies in the different sheets, prominence in each being given to the leading nation and its literature.

2. The *scale* necessarily varies—centuries marking the spaces of the earlier; periods of twenty-five or twenty years, of the later ages.

3. *Events* are recorded as nearly as possible on the line of their date; during the fifth century B.C. one sometimes inevitably crowds another out of its exact place.

4. *Names of Statesmen* are followed by dates indicating their tenure of power; added dates in brackets sometimes mark the duration of life.

5. *Names of Authors* are followed by dates of birth and death; in remote periods more frequently by single dates of the time when they are believed to have flourished.

6. *Names of Hebrew Prophets* are underlined and followed by figures marking the limits of the periods during which they are supposed to have prophesied.

It ought to be explicitly stated that the majority of the dates—especially of authors—in Table I. are traditional, and adopted on the basis of current conjecture. No attempt has been made to adjudicate on the controversies which surround them. Dates of like uncertainty in subsequent Tables are followed by a mark of interrogation (?). The accounts of "Sardanapalus" are so conflicting that his name has been inserted with a query in two distinct Tables. In Tables III. and IV. it has been found advisable to introduce colours—(1) In the Art columns; (2) In the History columns—to make more clear the relations of the contending nationalities. On the following principle they indicate—(1) The professions of the representative artists ; (2) The leading names, legal landmarks, and decisive victories of the most prominent peoples.

A. In the columns of Literature and Art:

PAINTERS, ...	RED.
SCULPTORS AND ARCHITECTS, ...	GREEN.
MUSICIANS, ...	BLUE.

B. In the columns of History :

GREEKS { ATHENIAN AND THEBAN,	.	.	BLUE.
{ SPARTAN AND SICILIAN,	.	.	BLUE BARS.
ROMANS, ...	.	.	RED.
PERSIANS, ...	.	.	RED BARS.
MACEDONIANS AND SUCCESSORS OF ALEXANDER,	.		GREEN.
PHŒNICIANS AND CARTHAGINIANS,	.	.	GREEN BARS.

Mr. Nichol has gratefully to acknowledge kind advice and assistance more especially received from Professor Sellar of Edinburgh, and Professor Ward of Owen's College, Manchester.

NOTE.—In Table II., for "Philanthus," read "Phalanthus."

CONTENTS.

TABLES OF ANCIENT LITERATURE AND HISTORY.

I. B.C. 1500 TO B.C. 750. FROM THE EXODUS TO THE FOUNDATION OF ROME. BY CENTURIES.

NOTE.—*The following dates have been assigned to important events or traditions previous to B.C. 1500:—*

I. BIBLICAL, ... The Deluge, 2348 B.C. Birth of Abram, 1996; of Esau and Jacob, 1837. Joseph in Egypt, 1729-1635. Birth of Moses, 1571.
II. ASSYRIA & EGYPT, Babel. Nimrod. Asshur, 2230. Nineveh. Ninus. Semiramis, 2180. Menes, 2700. Egyptian Thebes founded, 2280. Hyksos in Egypt, 1800-1600.
III. GREECE, ... Foundation of Sicyon, 2088; of Argos (Inachus), 1856; of Athens (Cecrops), 1556; of Sparta (Lelex), 1516. Deucalion, 1503.
IV. PHŒNICIA, ... Foundation of Tyre and Sidon, 2750.

B.C.	Asia, Africa, &c.	Palestine.	Literature.	Greece.	B.C.
1500	Rameses III., Sesostris, or Ammon, 19th Egyptian Dynasty, 1485. Pharaohs powerful, 1500-900	The Exodus, 1491 Deaths of Moses, Aaron, and Miriam, 1452-51 Joshua divides Canaan, 1445 First Judge in Israel (Othniel), 1402		Foundation of Thebes (Cadmus), 1493 Dardanus, 1480 Danaus in Argos, 1460 Foundation of Ilium, 1425	1500
1400	Eglon, King of Moab.	Ehud, second Judge, 1394-1354 Wars with Amalekites, Jebusites, Moabites. Ruth, 1320	The Vedas. Book of Job. (Ewald.) Sanchuniathon.	Eleusinian Mysteries, 1383 War of Erectheus and Eumolpus. Foundation of Mycenæ, 1344 Perseus. Cyclopes.	1400
1300	Latinus in Italy, 1240	Wars with Philistines. Barak and Deborah, 1296-1256 Jael and Sisera, 1296 War with Midianites. Gideon, 1249-1209 Abimelech, 1209-1206	Mythical Hymnology (Linus), 1280 Early Minstrelsy (Orpheus), 1260	Pelops, 1283 Calydonian Chase (Atalanta). Hercules. Minos in Crete, 1256 Argonautic Expedition, 1200-1240 Theseus in Athens, 1234 Seven against Thebes, 1220-1210 Agamemnon. Menelaus.	1300
1200	Proteus in Egypt.	Eli, High Priest, 1171-1165 War with Ammonites, 1161-1143	Dawn of Religious Epic (Mus...)	THE TROJAN WAR, 1192-1183 Return of the Chief...	1200

	Æneas in Italy. Alba Longa founded, ... 1152	War with Ammonites, ... 1161-1143 Shibboleth of Gilead. JEPHTHAH, ... 1143-1137 Wars with Philistines. SAMSON, ... 1140-1120 **SAMUEL**, ... 1141-1112		Dawn of Religious Epic (Musæus), 1180	[illegible] Orestes in Argos, ... 1176 Lydians on the sea, ... 1169 Æolian Migration, ... 1124 Thessaly settled, ... 1124 Dorian Migration. RETURN OF HERACLIDÆ, ... 1104 Melanthus in Athens, . . . 1104	
1100	Cheops (Gt. Pyramid), ... 1082 Mycerinus (Egypt). Hiram of Tyre, ... 1014 Queen of Sheba. TYRE great, ... 1000-586	**SAUL** (1st King), ... 1095-1056 **DAVID**, ... 1056-1015 **SOLOMON**, ... 1015-975		Psalms of David.	Pelasgi on the sea, ... 1077 Aletes in Corinth. . . . . 1074 Colony from Chalcis to CUMÆ, 1050 CODRUS in Athens, ... 1045 IONIC MIGRATION, ... 1044 Settlement of Peloponnesus. War between Chalcis and Eretria.	1100
1000	Shishak (Egypt) invades Judea, 972 Tartessus founded by Tyre. Benhadad I. (Damascus) allied with Asa. Benhadad II. ,, besieges Samaria, 901-892 Jezabel of Sidon marries Ahab.	Building of TEMPLE, ... 1012-1005 Revolt of Ten Tribes, ... 975 **JUDAH.** REHOBOAM, 975-958 Abijam, . . . 958-955 Asa, ... 955-914 Jehosaphat, . 914-889	**ISRAEL.** JEROBOAM I., 975-954 Nadab, . . . 954-953 Baasha, . . . 953-930 Elah, ... 930-929 Zimri, ... 929 Omri, ... 929-918 AHAB, ... 918-897	Proverbs of Solomon. Song of Solomon. HOMER, . . . fl. 962-927 Iliad and Odyssey, . . . 940-927 Creophylus (Samos).	Thracians on the sea, . . . 992 Alexas in Thessaly. Rhodians on the sea, ... 913	1000
900	Foundation of **CARTHAGE**, . . 878 Sardanapalus, ... 875 ? Revolt of Arbaces the Mede. Hazael attacks Israel, . . . 860 Benhadad III., ... 840 Syria tributary to Israel.	Jehoram, . . 889-885 Ahaziah, . . 885-884 Athaliah, . . 884-878 Jehoash, . . 878-839 Amaziah, . . 839-810	ELIJAH, . . 910-896 Ahaziah, . . 897-896 Joram, . . 896-884 ELISHA, . . 896-838 JEHU, . . 884-856 Jehoahaz, . 856-839 Joash, . . 839-826 JEROBOAM II., 825-784	Jonah (I.), ... c. 862 HESIOD (Ascra), ... 850 Joel (J.), ... 800	Phrygians on the sea, . . . 890 OLYMPIC GAMES, ... 884 LYCURGUS in Sparta, . . . 884 Settlement of Lacedæmon, 884-776 Cyprians on the sea, ... 865 Phœnicians on the sea, . . . 832 Foundation of Rhegium, . . 812 Æolian colonies, ... 800 Ionian colonies, ... 794	900
800 750	Egyptians on the sea, . . 787-751 Pul of Assyria invades Israel, . 770 Etruscans in Campania, . . . 760 Foundation of **ROME**, . . . 753	Uzziah (or Azariah), 810-758 Jotham, . . 758-742	*Interregnum.* Zechariah, . . . 773 Shallum, ... 772 Menahem, . 772-761 Pekahiah, . 761-759 Pekah, . . 759-739	Amos (I.), ... c. 787 Hosea (I.), ... c. 785 Agias of Troezen, ... 776 Stasinus (Cyprus). Arctinus (Miletus), . . 775-740 Cinæthon (Lacedæmon), . . fl. 765 Eumelus (Corinth), . . 760-730	VICTORY OF CORŒBUS, . . 776 Argos heads a Confederacy, . 774 Pandosia and Metapontum founded, 774 Pheidon of Argos, . . . 780-740 MILETUS powerful. Colonies, 750 Decennial ARCHONS at Athens, 753	800 750

II. B.C. 750 TO B.C. 500. FROM FOUNDATION OF ROME TO BEGINNING OF ROMAN REPUBLIC.

BY PERIODS OF TWENTY-FIVE YEARS.

B.C.	Asia and Africa	Palestine	Literature and Art	Greece	Italy and Sicily	B.C.
750	Nabonasar (Babylon), . 747 Persians besiege Nineveh, . 747 Tiglath Pileser destroys Syria, and carries 2½ tribes captive, . . . 740 Shalmaneser (Assyria) invades Israel, . . . 728	Pekah and Rezon of Syria besiege Jerusalem, . 742 Ahaz, of Judah, . . 742-726 *Interregnum in Israel.* Hoshea, of Israel, . 730-721 HEZEKIAH, of Judah, 726-698	Micah (J.). . . . c. 750-710 ISAIAH, ... fl. 747-698	Rise of CORINTH, . . 745 First Messenian War, 743-723 Chalcis founds Naxos, . 735 Corinthian Colonies— Corcyra, ... 734 PHILOLAUS of Thebes, . 728	ROMULUS, . . 753-716 War with Sabines, . 750 Union „ . . 747 Romulus and Acron, 1st Spolia Opima. SYRACUSE founded, . 734 Leontium and Catana founded, 730	750
725	Sargon captures Israel, . 721 Gyges in Lydia, . . 716-679 Sennacherib invades Judah, 713 „ destroyed, . 710 Deioces in Media, . 709-657	CAPTIVITY OF ISRAEL, 721 MANASSEH, . . 698-643	NAHUM, . . . fl. 720-698 Lesches (Lesbos), . . 710 Archilochus (Paros), . . 708	Achæans found Sybaris, 721 War between Sparta and Argos, 718 Achæans found Croton, . 710	NUMA POMPILIUS, . 716-673 Religious Laws. TARENTUM founded (Philanthus), 708	725
700	Esarhaddon of Nineveh takes Babylon, . . . 680 Esarhaddon colonizes Samaria, . . . 677	Idolatry in Judah.	Simonides (Amorgus), . 693-662 Tyrtæus (Sparta), . . 685 Callinus, ... 678 Terpander (Lesbos) crowned at Musical Contest, . 676	Annual ARCHONS at Athens, 683 Second Messenian War, 685-668		700
675	Psammetichus (Egypt), 671-617 Colony of Naucratis, . 665 Phraortes (Media), . 656-635	War of Holofernes, . 656? Judith ?	BUDDHA ? Alcman (Sparta), . . 670 Thaletas (Pyrrhic songs), . 670 Eucheir and Eugrammus, . 660 Temple of Zeus at Elis, . 660	Rise of Megara, . . . 670 Sea-fight, Corinth and Corcyra, 665 Byzantium founded, . . 657 Orthagoras in Sicyon, . . 657 Cypselus at Corinth, . . 655 Bacchiadæ expelled, . . 655	TULLUS HOSTILIUS, . 673-640 Destruction of Alba, . . 665 Messana founded, . . 660 Zaleucus in Locri, . . 660	675
650	CYRENE founded, . . 641 Cyaxares, . . . 634-595 Scythians in Asia, . 634-607	Amon, ... 643-641 JOSIAH, . . . 641-610 „ repairs the Temple, 624	ZEPHANIAH, . . fl. 640-609 JEREMIAH, . . „ 628-586 THALES, . . . 644-548	Voyages of Colæus and Corobius. Colony of Battus to Cyrene, 641 Sinope founded, . . 640	ANCUS MARTIUS, . 640-616 Ostia founded, . . 640	650

Period					
625					**625**
600					**600**
575					**575**
550					**550**
525					**525**
500					**500**

Egypt — Persia — Carthage

Pharaoh Necho circumnavigates Africa, . . . 615?
Pharaoh Necho invades Judah, 610
Nebuchadnezzar sacks Tyre, 586
　" takes Jerusalem, 606-598
Sardanapalus?
Fall of Nineveh, . 606 or 597?
Pharaoh Hophra (or Apries), 595-570
Astyages or Ahasuerus, 595-560
Siege of Sidon.
Civil War in Egypt.
Periplus of Hanno, . . 570?
Voyage of Himilco, . . 570?
CYRUS King of Persia, 559-530
Crœsus in Lydia, . . 560-546
Amasis (Egypt), . . 570-526
Belshazzar or Labynetus. Babylon taken, . . . 536
Mago. Carthaginian Colonies.
Cambyses (Ahasuerus), . 529-523
Psammenitus (Egypt), . 525
Persian Conquest of Egypt, 525
DARIUS Hystaspes, . . 521-486
Periplus of Scylax.
Carthage a Republic.
Sea-fight with Phocæa.
Siege of Naxos by Aristagoras, 501

Judah

Passover. Ark restored, . 623
Jehoahaz, ... 610
JEHOIAKIM, . . . 610-599
CAPTIVITY OF JUDAH, seventy years, . . . 606-536
Jechoniah, ... 599
ZEDEKIAH, . . . 599-588
Return of Jews, subject to Cyrus, 536
Zerubbabel, Governor, . 536
Second Temple built, . 535-515

Era of Seven Sages—

[Thales, Bias, Pittacus, Solon, Cleobulus, Periander, Chilon.]
Arion, ... 625-610
Stesichorus (Himera), . 612
SAPPHO (Lesbos), . . 610
HABAKKUK, . . fl. 612-598
Epimenides in Athens, . 597
ALCÆUS (Lesbos), . . 604
Anaximander, . . 611-547
Anacharsis in Athens, . 592
DANIEL, . . fl. 606-534
OBADIAH, . . " 588-583
Susarion, . . . fl. 578
Later Psalms.
EZEKIEL, . . fl. 595-536
The Dædalidæ, . . 570
Chersiphron, . . fl. 560
CONFUCIUS. ZOROASTER. ?
Æsop, . . . fl. 560
Euganon (Cyrene), . . 560
ANACREON (Teos), . . 560
Pherecydes and Phocylides.
Anaximenes, . . fl. 548
Theognis (Megara), . . 541
Xenophanes (Colophon), . 538
Ibycus (Rhegium), . . 540
PYTHAGORAS, . . fl. 531
Thespis (Attica). . . 535
HAGGAI, . . fl. 520-518
ZECHARIAH, . . " 520-518
Phrynichus, . . fl. 412
PARMENIDES, . . fl. 505
HERACLITUS (Ephesus), fl. 505
CORINNA (Tanagra), . 500
Myrtis, ... 500

Greece

DRACO at Athens, . . 621
Cylon " . . . 620
PITTACUS at Mitylene, . 611
Cleisthenes at Sicyon, . 600-560
Alcæus exiled, . . . 590
First Sacred War, . 595-585
SOLON at Athens, . . 594
Cypselid dynasty ends, . 581
Elis subdues Pisa, . . 572
PEISISTRATUS at Athens, 560-527
Nile opened to Greeks.
Polycrates at Samos, . 532-522
Hipparchus slain, . . 514
Hippias rules, . . . 514
EXPULSION OF PEISISTRATIDÆ, 510
CLEISTHENES at Athens, . 510
Cleomenes at Sparta, . 519-490
Embassy of Aristagoras, . 500

Rome

TARQUINIUS PRISCUS, . 616-578
Massilia founded, . . 600
SERVIUS TULLIUS, . 578-534
Census. Comitia Centuriata at Rome.
Phalaris of Agrigentum, 570-554
Pythagoras at Croton, . 540-510
TARQUINIUS SUPERBUS, 534-509
Roman Kingdom extended over Latium.
Wars of Syracuse and Gela.
Croton destroys Sybaris, . 510
Porsenna at Rome, . . 509
Commercial Treaty with Carthage, . . . 508
1st Valerian Laws, . . 508

III. B.C. 500 to B.C. 323. FROM FOUNDATION OF ROMAN REPUBLIC TO DEATH OF ALEXANDER. BY PERIODS OF TWENTY-FIVE YEARS.

B.C.	Greece.	Sicily, Asia, Africa.	Literature and Art.	Rome.	B.C.
500	War between Athens and Ægina, 491 Heralds from Darius, 491 Persian Fleet wrecked off Athos, 492 MILTIADES, . . fl. 515-489 ” at Athens, 493-489 Battle of MARATHON, . 490 ARISTIDES, fl. 489-483 and 479-468 THEMISTOCLES (514-447),fl.480-471 Athenian Fleet built, 481: Walls, 478 LEONIDAS at THERMOPYLÆ, . 480 Artemisium, SALAMIS, . 480 PLATÆA and MYCALE, . 479 PAUSANIAS, . . fl. 479-471 Growth of ATHENIAN EMPIRE, 478-445	Ionian Revolt, . . 501-493 Siege of Naxos, . . 501 Persia recovers Cyprus, 498 Histiæus sent to the Coast, 496 Battle of Lade. Miletus taken, 494 Mardonius subdues Macedonia, 492 Carthaginians in Sicily. XERXES I. reigns, . 485-465 Egyptian Revolt, . . 486-484 GELON at SYRACUSE, . 485-477 BATTLE of HIMERA, . 480 Theron at Agrigentum, . 488-472 HIERO I. at Syracuse, . 478-475 Pausanias at Byzantium, . 477	ÆSCHYLUS, . . 524-456 Ageladas (Argos), . . fl. 500 Hecatæus, . . ” 500 Epicharmus (Sicily), . ” 490 Simonides (Ceos), . . ” 490 Pherecydes (historian), . ” 480 PINDAR, . . 522-442 Hegesias and Hegias. Leucippus—Atomic Theory. Hellanicus (Mitylene), . 496-411	CONSULAR Government at Rome, 508-60 Battle of Lake Regillus, . 498 1st Secession to Mons Sacer, 494 TRIBUNES of the Pleb, . 494 SPURIUS CASSIUS, . 494-483 LATIN LEAGUE, . . 493 Volscian War (Coriolanus), . 489 Hernican League, . . 488 Agrarian Law of Cassius, . 486 Wars with Veii, . . 481-475 Expedition of the Fabii, . 477 Fabii destroyed at Cremera, . 475	500
475	Ostracism of Themistocles, . 471 Death of Pausanias, . . 471 Argives take Mycenæ, . 468 Athenians at Naxos, . . 466 Battle of Eurymedon, . 466 Revolt of Thasos, . . 465-463 Revolt of the Helots, . 464 THIRD MESSENIAN WAR, . 464-455 Ithome taken, . . 455 CIMON . fl. 466-461 and 454-449 Laws of Pericles and Ephialtes, 461 Long Walls built, . . 457-456 Athenian Victory at Œnophyta, 456 Tolmides sails round Malea, . 455 Five Years' Truce, . . 450	Victories of Cimon, . . 476 NAVAL Victory of Hiero over Tuscans, . . 474 SYRACUSE free, . . 466-405 ARTAXERXES I. (Ahasuerus), 465-425 Story of ESTHER, . . 461-451 Themistocles in Persia, . 465-447 Egyptian War with Persia, . 460-455 Athenians in Egypt, . . 460 AGRIGENTUM powerful, . 470-405 EZRA, Governor in Judæa, . 458-449	ANAXAGORAS, . . 500-428 Diogenes of Apollonia, . fl. 468 Zeno of Elea, . . ” 464 SOPHOCLES, . . 495-406 ” Tragic Victory, . ” 468 Polygnotus (Stoa Poicile), . fl. 460 Ion of Chios, . . ” 451 Bacchylides, . . ” 450 Archelaus (Physicus), . ” 450 Phormio, . . ” 450 Crates, Cratinus, Eupolis, . ” 450 Phrynis, . . ” 456 DEMOCRITUS (Abdera), . ” 450	1st PUBLILIAN LAWS, . . 471 Antium taken, . . 470 Suicide of Appius Claudius, . 470 Terentilian Bill, . . 462 Æquian War (Cincinnatus), . 458 Icilian Law, . . 454 Commissioners to Greece, . 453 THE DECEMVIRATE, . 451-449 THE TWELVE TABLES, . 450	478
450	PERICLES, . . (499-429) ” in power, . . 459-429 Second Sacred War, . . 448 Athenian defeat at Coronea, . 447 Thirty Years' Truce, . . 445 Revolt of Eubœa and Megara, 445 Decline of Athenian Empire, 445-404 War of Corinth and Corcyra, . 435 Congress at Lacedæmon, . 433 PELOPONNESIAN WAR, . 431-405 Invasion of Attica by Archidamus, 431 Plague at Athens, . . 430-429 Death of Pericles, . . 429 Siege of Platæa, . . 429-427 Naval Victories of Phormio, . 429 Corcyrean Massacre, . . 427 Demosthenes in Ætolia, . 426 Sphacteria taken, . . 425	Athenian Victory at Salamis in Cyprus, . . 449 Syracuse subdues Agrigentum, 446 ” defeats Etruscans, . 446 Athenian Colony to Thurii, . 444 CARTHAGINIAN VOYAGES. NEHEMIAH Governor in Judæa, 445-420 The Samian War, . . 440-439 Carthaginians in Sicily, . 431 Revolt of Lesbos, . . 428 Fall of Mitylene, . . 427 41 Ships from Athens to Sicily, 426	PHIDIAS (Parthenon), . fl. 448-440 Polycleitus and Myron, . fl. 440 HERODOTUS, . . 484-408 EURIPIDES, . . 480-406 Melissus (Samos), . . fl. 444 EMPEDOCLES (Agrigentum), . fl. 444 Alcamenes, . . fl. 440 METON (astronomer), . . fl. 433 Era of the Sophists. PROTAGORAS, . . fl. 444 Prodicus, . . ” 444 GORGIAS, . . ” 430 MALACHI (Judæa), . . fl. 430-420 Erechtheium rebuilt, . 433-393 Diagoras (ἄθεος), . . ” 425 Cinesias, . . ” 425	APPIUS CLAUDIUS (Virginia) (Dentatus), . . 449 2nd Secession to Mons Sacer, 448 Valerian and Horatian Laws, . 448 3rd Secession to Mons Sacer, 445 Canuleian Laws, . . 445 CONSULAR TRIBUNES, . 444 CENSORS at Rome, . . 443 Famine at Rome, . . 440 Death of Spurius Mælius, . 439 Cornelius Cossus and Lars Tol- umnius, 2nd Spolia Opima, . 437 Destruction of Fidenæ, . 426	430
425	CLEON, . . fl. 425-422 ALCIBIADES, fl. 424-413 and 411-404	DARIUS II., Nothus, . . 424-405 Congress of Sicilians at Gela, . 424	Antiphon, . . 480-411 Philolaus ?	Twenty Years' Truce with Veii.	425

BRASIDAS at Amphipolis, . . 422
Peace of Nicias, . . 421-415
Battle of Mantinea, . . 418
Alcibiades at Argos, . . 418
Affair of Melos, . . 416
Agis occupies Decelea, . . 413
Fleet destroyed at Syracuse, . 413
The 400 at Athens, . . 411
Callicratidas defeated at Arginusæ.
  Generals executed, . . 406
Battle of Ægospotami, . . 405
LYSANDER enters Athens, . 404
Critias and Thirty Tyrants, . 404

400

Democracy restored (Thrasybulus), 403
Socrates condemned, . . 399
Coalition against Sparta, . . 395
Lysander slain, . . 395
Corinthian War, . . 394-392
2nd Battle of Coronea, . . 394
Long Walls restored by CONON, 394
Battle of Lechæum, . . 383
Agesilaus in Acarnania, . . 391
OLYNTHIAN WAR, . . 383-379
HEIGHT OF SPARTAN POWER.
Victories of PELOPIDAS, . 378-364
Athenians allied with Thebes, . 378
EPAMINONDAS, . . 371-362

378

Battle of LEUCTRA, . . 371
SUPREMACY OF THEBES.
Agesilaus in Arcadia, . . 370
Alexander of Pheræ in Thessaly, 370
Theban Invasions of Laconia,
. . . 369, 368, 362
Pelopidas in Thessaly, . . 368
The Tearless Victory, . . 367
Battle of MANTINEA, . . 362
PHILIP II. of Macedon. . 359-336
Social War, . . 357-355
1st Sacred or PHOCIAN WAR, 355-346
Siege of Methone, . . 353

380

Olynthus taken by Philip, . 348
Philip of Macedon in Thrace, . 341
2nd Sacred or LOCRIAN WAR, 339
Battle of CHÆRONEA, . . 338
ALEXANDER III., 336-323
Destruction of Thebes, . . 335
MACEDONIAN EMPIRE, . 334-143
Battle of Granicus, . . 334
  "   Issus, . . 333
  "   Arbela, . . 331
Exile of Demosthenes. . 324
Death of Alexander, . . 323

325

Catana, . . 415
SYRACUSAN EXPEDITION, 415-413
GYLIPPUS arrives at Syracuse. 413
Athenian Allies revolt, . 412-411
PERSIAN TREATIES WITH PELO-
PONNESUS, . . 412-411
Revolt at Samos. Alcibiades, 412-411
THRASYBULUS with Athenian Fleet,
. . . 411
Battle of Cynossema, . . 411
ARTAXERXES II., . . 405-359
Expedition of CYRUS the Younger, 401

400

Return of the 10,000 Greeks, . 400
DIONYSIUS I. of Syracuse, 405-368
Agesilaus in Asia, . . 396-395
CONON at Cnidus, . . 394
Victory of Dionysius at Helorus, 389
Peace of Antalcidas, . . 387
Cyprian War, . . 385-375
Defeat of Evagoras, . . 385
WARS OF SYRACUSE AND CARTHAGE,
. . . 410-340
Hamilcar and Mago.
BITHYNIAN KINGDOM, . 378-75
Carthaginians in Italy, . . 379
Timotheus in Asia, . . 372

378

Plato in Sicily, . . 370
Embassy of Pelopidas to Persia, 367
DIONYSIUS II. of Syracuse, 368-343
Joshua slain by High Priest, . 366
Plato's 2nd Visit to Sicily, . 361
Samaritans build Temple at
Gerizim, . . 360
Kingdom of PONTUS, . 360-66
ARTAXERXES III., Ochus, 359-338
Revolt of Artabazus, . . 354
Dion at Syracuse, . . 357-354
Sidon destroyed, . . 351

380

TIMOLEON at Syracuse, 345-337
HANNO in Carthage. . 340
DARIUS III., . . 336-330
FALL OF TYRE, . . 332
Foundation of ALEXANDRIA, . 332
BABYLON taken by Alexander, 331
Persepolis burnt . . 331
Judæa subject to Alexander, . 330
Darius slain by Bessus, . . 330
Alexander at the Hyphasis, . 327
Alexander at Susa, . . 325
Voyage of Nearchus, . . 324-323

325

SOCRATES, . . 468-399
LYSIAS, . . 459-380
ARISTOPHANES, . . 444-380
  "The Clouds," . . 423
AMOCLES, . . 440-390
Agathon, . . fl. 415
HIPPOCRATES, . . 460-357
Callimachus, . . fl. 412
XENOPHON, . . 444-362
PARRHASIUS, . . fl. 400
Melanippides, . . fl. 400

400

Euclid of Megara, . . fl. 400
Antisthenes, . . 426-371
Aristippus, . . 400-365
PLATO, . . 429-347
ISOCRATES, . . 436-338
Timanthes, . . fl. 385
Timotheus, . . 446-357
Scopas, . . c. 395-350
Isæus, . . 420-350
Diogenes the Cynic, . . 419-324
Xenocrates, . . 396-314
Speusippus, . . d. 319

378

Archytas (Tarentum), . . 370
Eudoxus (mathematician), . 367
Phocion, . . 402-317
"Ludi Scenici" at Rome, . 365
PRAXITELES, . . fl. 360
Pamphilus, . . " 360
ÆSCHINES, . . 389-314
DEMOSTHENES, . 382-322
Æneas Tacticus, . . fl. 360
ARISTOTLE, . . 384-322

380

Cleomenes, . . fl. 350
Protogenes (Rhodes), . 360-300
Lycurgus (Athens), . . fl. 340
Lysippus, . . fl. 335
APELLES (Cos), . . 350-308
PYRRHO, . . fl. 350
Hypereides, . . " 346
Demades, . . " 330
Deinarchus, . . " 324
Theopompus (historian), 378-305
Diphilus and Philemon, . fl. 330
MENANDER, . . 342-291

325

Æquian Wars, . . 419-409
Colonies—Bola, Lavici, Feren-
tinum, Anxur.
Victories over Volscians, . 409-406
Plebeian Questors, . . 409
Pay in Army, . . 406
Siege of Veii (Camillus), . 405-396

400

Embassy to Delphi, . . 398
Battle of the ALLIA, . . 390
ROME BURNT by the Gauls
(Brennus), . . 390
M. F. CAMILLUS Dictator, . 390
ROME REBUILT, . . 389
Execution of M. Manlius, . 384
Recovery of Revolted Towns
—Tusculum, Præneste, An-
tium, &c., . . 383-377
LICINIAN LAWS, . . 377-367

378

PRÆTORS and Curule Ædiles at
Rome, . . 366
1st Plebeian CONSUL, . . 366
Plague at Rome. Death of
Camillus, . . 365
Legend of M. Curtius, . . 365
Wars with Gauls, Etruscans,
and Hernicans, . . 362-349
Legends of Manlius Torquatus
and Valerius Corvus.
Laws of Debt, . . 357, 352, 347
C. Marcius Rutilus, 1st Plebeian
Dictator, . . 356
C. Marcius Rutilus, 1st Plebeian
Censor, . . 351

380

Treaty with Carthage, . . 348
1st SAMNITE WAR, . . 343-341
Battle of Mt. Gaurus, . . 343
Mutiny at Lautulæ, . . 342
Genucian Laws, . . 342
LATIN WAR, . . 340-338
Battle of Mt. Vesuvius (Devotion
of P. Decius Mus I.), . 340
2nd PUBLILIAN LAWS, . . 339
1st Plebeian Prætor, . . 337
Settlement of LATIUM, . 338-328
Servitude for debt abolished, . 326

325

BY PERIODS OF TWENTY-FIVE YEARS.

B.C.	Rome and Carthage	Literature and Art	Greece	Sicily, Asia, Egypt, &c. (SUCCESSORS OF ALEXANDER)	B.C.
323	2nd SAMNITE WAR, . 326-304 Caudine Forks, . 321 C. POSTUS of Telesia, fl. 321-292 Battle of Lautulæ, . 315 Roman Victory at Cinna, . 314 ETRUSCAN WAR, . 311-309 L. Papirius Cursor Dictator, 310 Q. Fabius crosses Ciminian Hills; defeats Tuscans at Vadimon. Bomilcar at Carthage, . 308 APPIUS CLAUDIUS Censor, 312-308 Bovianum taken, . 305 Ogulnian Law, . 300	EUCLID (Alexandria), . fl. 325 MANETHO, Egyptian Historian, fl. 320 Pytheas (navigator)? Philippides, . fl. 320 Chares (Lindus), . fl. 320 Euhemerus, . fl. 320 Polemo, Crates, Crantor, . fl. 315 TIMÆUS (Tauromenium), 352-257 Diocles, Roman hist. (Peparethus)? APPIAN WAY AND AQUEDUCT, 312 Demetrius Phalereus, . 345-28, Eudemus, . fl. 300	Perdiccas Regent, . 323-321 Antipater in Macedonia, 323-318 Lysimachus in Thrace, 323-281 Cassander in Greece, 317-296 The Lamian War (Leosthenes), Death of Demosthenes, 323-322 Cassander takes Athens, 322 Philip III. (Arrhidæus) killed, 317 Olympias killed by Cassander, 316 Roxana and Son killed, 311 DEMETRIUS Poliorcetes at Athens, 308-304 and 295-290 at Thebes, 293-291	Ptolemy in Egypt, . 322-285 Antigonus in Syria, . 323-301 Eumenes (Cappadocia), 323-315 Seleucus at Babylon, 321 and 312-280 PTOLEMY in Egypt, . 322-30 Ptolemy I (Soter) takes Jerusalem, 320 War of Antigonus and Eumenes, 320-315 AGATHOCLES at Syracuse, 317-289 defeated at Himera, 310 Naval War at Cyprus and Rhodes, 307-305 Battle of IPSUS, . 301	325
300	3rd SAMNITE WAR (Samnites, Etruscans, Umbrians, Gauls), 298-290 Gellius Egnatius, Samnite leader. Battle of SENTINUM (D. Mus II), 295 Execution of C. Pontius, . 292 Last Secession (Janiculum), 286 HORTENSIAN Law, . 286 Renewed Etruscan & Gallic War, 283 2nd Battle of Lake Vadimon, 283 War with Tarentum, . 281 PYRRHUS invades Italy, 281-275 Battle of Heraclea, . 280 Battle of ASCULUM (D. Mus III), 279 Rome and Carthage allied, 279	THEOPHRASTUS, . 374-287 Capitoline Wolf, . 29. ZENO, the Stoic (Citium), 366-264 EPICURUS, . 341-270 Appius Claudius Cæcus 1st Roman Orator, . fl. 280 Zoilus and Zenodotus, . 28. Hegesias (Cyrene), . 28. THEOCRITUS, . 28. Bion and Moschus, . 270 ARISTARCHUS (Astronomer), fl. 280-267 SEPTUAGINT, . 277.	Philip IV., of Macedon, 297-296 Demetrius Poliorcetes in Macedon, 294-287 PYRRHUS of Epirus, 318-272 reigned, 306-272 in Macedon, 287-286 in Italy and Sicily, 281-275 Death of Demetrius Poliorcetes, 283 Gauls in Greece, 280, 279, 278 Brennus at Delphi, . 278 ÆTOLIAN LEAGUE, 284-167	SELEUCIDÆ in Syria, 312-64 Sandracottus' Indian Empire, 312-160 Rhodes powerful, . 300-200 Kingdom of Pergamus, 283-133 Lysimachus defeated and slain by Seleucus at Corupedion, 281 Ptolemy II. (Philadelphus), 285-247 Gauls settled in Galatia, 277 GREAT WALL OF CHINA ?	300
278	Battle of BENEVENTUM, 275 Tarentum taken, . 272 SOUTH ITALY SUBDUED, 270-266 1st PUNIC WAR, . 264-241 Hiero of Syracuse joins Rome, 263 Agrigentum taken, . 262 Romans build a Fleet, . 261 Victory of Duilius at Mylæ, 260 Roman Naval Victory at Economus, 256 Regulus invades Africa, . 256 defeated by Xanthippus, 255 Carthalo recovers Agrigentum, 254 Roman Victory at Panormus, 250	Lycophron, . c. 285-247 Aratus (Astronomer), . fl. 270 Hieronymus (Cardia), . 270 ARCESILAUS (New Academy), 300-241 Callimachus (Alexandria), fl. 260. Columna Rostrata, . 260 Monumenta Scipionum, . 260 CLEANTHES, . 300-220	ACHÆAN LEAGUE, 280-146 Antigonus Gonatas recovers Macedon, . 272 takes Athens, . 268 ARATUS, . (271-213) at Sicyon, . 251	Extension of Alexandrian commerce Egyptian Embassy to Rome, 273 HIERO II. of Syracuse, 269-219 Rise of PARTHIA. The ARSACIDÆ, 256 to A.D. 226 Kingdom of BACTRIA, 254-126	278
280	Carthaginian Victory at Drepana, 249 Sieges of Lilybæum and Drepana,	ARCHIMEDES, . 287-212 ERATOSTHENES, . 270-196	Aratus, General of Achæan League, 245 at Corinth and Megara, 243	Dynasty of Tsin in China, 250-206 Ptolemy III. (Euergetes), 247-222	280

	War of Carthaginians and Mercenaries, 241-238 Sardinia and Corsica seized, . 238 Temple of Janus closed, . . . 235 Agrarian Law of Flaminius, . 232 Illyrian War (Queen Teuta), . 229 HASDRUBAL founds Carthagena, 229 Gallic invasion (Boii and Insubres). Battle of Telamon, ... 225-223 Clastidium. Viridomarus & Marcellus. 3rd Spolia Opima, ... 222	LIVIUS ANDRONICUS, . fl. 240-214 1st Tragedies at Rome, . . 240-235 Cn NÆVIUS, ... fl. 235-202 Sosilus and Silanus.	Antigonus Doson in Macedon, 233-221 Athens joins Achæan League, . 229 Roman Embassy to Greece, . 228 War between Cleomenes of Sparta and Achæan League, . . 227-222 Reforms of Cleomenes, . . 226-225	Attalus I. (Pergamus), . . 241-197 ,, defeats Galatians, . 241 Sicily 1st Roman Province, . 241 Gallia Cisalpina a Roman Province, ... 222	
225	HANNIBAL, . . (247-183) Siege of Saguntum, ... 219 2nd Illyrian War, ... 219 2nd PUNIC WAR, . . . 218-202 Hannibal crosses the Alps, . . 218 Ticinus and Trebia, ... 218 Battle of TRASIMENE, . . . 217 Battle of CANNÆ, ... 216 Revolt of Capua, ... 216-211 Fabius and Marcellus. Nola, . 215 Scipios defeated by HASDRUBAL, 212 Hannibal before Rome, . . . 211 Battle of METAURUS. Nero, . 208 P. CORNELIUS SCIPIO in Africa, 204 Syphax and Massinissa, . . . 204 Hannibal leaves Italy, . . . 203 Battle of ZAMA, ... 202	Q. Fabius Pictor, . . . } Cincius Alimentus, . . } fl. 220 Apollonius Rhodius, . . . 238-188 PLAUTUS, ... 253-184 Greek Works of Art brought to Rome, ... 212 ENNIUS, ... 239-169 CÆCILIUS Statius, . . . d. 168 Rise of PHARISEES and SADDUCEES. Hermippus (Smyrna) ? Philinus of Agrigentum, . . fl. 200	Battle of Sellasia, ... 221 Aratus and Antigonus take Sparta, 221 PHILIP V., Macedon, . . 221-179 Philip and Achæans against Ætolians, 221-217 Philip allied with Hannibal, . 216 Rome ,, Ætolians, . 211 PHILOPŒMEN, General of Achæan League, ... 208-183 Peace with Ætolians and Rome, 205 Philip's War with Rome, . 200-197	ANTIOCHUS the Great (Syria), 224-187 Ptolemy IV. (Philopator), . 222-205 Hasdrubal assassinated in Spain, 220 First Commercial War— Byzantium and Rhodes, . . 214 Siege of Syracuse, . . . 214-212 Battle of Anitorgis, ... 212 ,, Elinga, ... 208 Ptolemy V., ... 205-181 Attalus and Rhodians war with Philip, ... 203 Antiochus conquers Palestine, . 203	225
200	1st Macedonian War, . . 200-197 T. Quintius Flamminius, . . fl. 197 Hannibal with Antiochus, . . 196 Ligurian Wars, 200, 193, 181, &c. WAR WITH ANTIOCHUS, . 191-190 Ætolian War, ... 191-190 Deaths of Hannibal and Scipio, 183 Encroachments of Massinissa, 182-174 Villian Law, ... 181 M. PORCIUS CATO, . . (234-149) T. Sempronius Gracchus in Spain, 179	ROSETTA STONE, ... 197 PACUVIUS, ... 220-130 AFRANIUS, ... fl. 175 Titinius. Trabea. Atilius. CATO, ... fl. 170 CARNEADES (Cyrene), . . 213-129 POLYBIUS, ... 207-122	Battle of CYNOSCEPHALÆ, . . 197 Flaminius proclaims Freedom of Greece at the Isthmian Games, 196 Philopœmen defeats Nabis of Sparta, ... 192 Sparta joins Achæan League, . 192 Antiochus in Greece, . . . 192 Philopœmen abrogates Laws of Lycurgus, ... 188 LYCORTAS General of Achæan League, 183 Embassy of Callicrates, . . . 179 PERSEUS of Macedon, . . 179-168	Prusias of Bithynia, . . . 200-180 Eumenes II., Pergamus, . 197-158 Dynasty of Han in China. Battle of MAGNESIA, . . . 190 Hannibal at Court of Prusias, . 183 Ptolemy VI., ... 181-146 Pharnaces of Pontus cedes Paphlagonia to Rome, . . 179 Antiochus Epiphanes, . . 176-165	200
175	Eumenes II. comes to Rome, . 172 2nd Macedonian War, . . 171-168 1000 Achæans in prison at Rome, 167-151 L. Æmilius Paulus, . . . fl. 168 Romans intervene in Egypt, . 161 Embassy of Carneades, Diogenes, and Critolaus, ... 155 War in Spain, ... 153-152 War with Andriscus, ... 148 3rd PUNIC WAR, . . . 149-146 ACHÆAN WAR, ... 147-146 P. Cornelius Scipio Minor, . fl. 146 DESTRUCTION OF CARTHAGE, 146	TERENTIUS Afer (Carthage), 195-159 Zeno (historian), ... fl. 160 HIPPARCHUS, ... ,, 160 Calpurnius Piso, ... ,, 160 Sempronius Tuditanus, . . ,, 160 Cassius Hemina, ... ,, 160 Cn Gellius, ... ,, 160 Aristarchus (Grammarian), . . 156 Apollodorus (Grammarian), . 146	War of Perseus and Rome, 171-168 Battle of PYDNA, ... 168 Athenians attack Oropus. ,, fined by Rome, . . 155 Andriscus in Macedonia, . . 149 Achæan War with Rome, . 147-146 Diæus defeated at Leucopetra, 146 DESTRUCTION OF CORINTH (Mummius), ... 146 Greece constituted a Roman Province (Achaia), . . . 146-145	War of Antiochus and Egypt, 172-168 Revolt of Jews under Mattathias, 168 ASMONÆANS in Judæa, . . 168-37 Cyrene and Libya separate from Egypt, ... 164 Judas MACCABÆUS, . . . 166-161 ,, allies with Rome, . . . 161 Bactrians in India, ... 160 Jonathan MACCABÆUS, . . 161-143 Demetrius Soter and Alexander Balas. Judæa free with tribute to Syria.	175
150					150

BY PERIODS OF TWENTY-FIVE YEARS.

B.C.	Rome	Latin Literature	Other Nations	Other Literature and Art	B.C.
180	Lusitanian War, . . . 150-138	C. Laelius (phil.), . . . 186-	Polybius legislates for the Achæan Cities, ... 145	Antipater of Tarsus (Stoic).	180
	Death of Viriathus, . . . 140	A. Postumius Albinus (hist.), fl. 150	Demetrius Nicator (Syria), 145-141		
	Scipio Africanus (Minor) Censor, 142	P. Sempronius Asellio (hist.), fl. 130	Simon MACCABÆUS, . 143-136	PANÆTIUS, ... d. 111	
	Numantine War, . . . 143-133	Atius (dramatist), . . . 170-76	JUDÆA independent.	Glycon (sculptor).	
	Scipio takes and destroys Numantia, 133	The Gracchi (orators).	MACEDON formally absorbed by Rome.		
	TIBERIUS GRACCHUS, . (164-133)		Hyrcanus governs Judæa, 136-106		
		L. Caelius Antipater (jurist), fl. 125	Demetrius Nicator restored, in Parthia, . . . 131		
	Servile War in Sicily, . . 134-132		Demetrius Nicator restored, 130-126	Blossius of Cumæ (philosopher).	
	SEMPRONIAN LAWS, . . 133-123	M. Æmilius Scaurus (orator), 163-90	Attalus III. leaves Pergamus to Rome, . . . 130		
	GAIUS GRACCHUS, . . (154-121)	LUCILIUS, . . . 148-103	Hyrcanus subdues Idumea and Samaria, and destroys Temple at Gerizim, . . 129	RISE OF THE ESSENES.	
125	Fulvius Flaccus and L. Drusus popular leaders.		Roman Province in TRANSALPINE GAUL.		125
	Death of C. Gracchus, . 121		" Colony sent to Carthage, 123		
	Q. Metellus leader of Senate.		Parthians subdue Bactria, . 120		
	Sumptuary Laws.		Ptolemy Lathyrus and Alexander, 117-81		
	Cimbrian War, . . 113-101	Antonius (orator), . . 143-70	FIRST NORTHERN MIGRATIONS.		
	Jugurthine War, . . 111-106	Crassus (orator), . . 140-91			
	JUGURTHA captured, . . 106		Pharisees and Sadducees political factions, civil contests in Judæa.		
	2nd Servile War, . . 103-101		MITHRIDATES (Pontus), . 120-63		
	Marius conquers Teutones, Aquæ Sextiæ, ... 102		" conquests on Black Sea, 112-110	Archias (poet), . . . fl. 102	
	Marius conquers Cimbri, Vercellæ, 101	P. Rutilius Rufus (historian), fl. 100	" takes Galatia, . . 102	Hierocles (fabulist), . . " 102	
	C. MARIUS (157-86), 6th Consulship, 100	Q. Claudius Quadrigarius (hist.), " 100			
100	L. App. Saturninus Tribune, . 100	Artemidorus (Ephesus), . fl. 100	Ptolemy Apion leaves CYRENE to Rome, ... 96	Antipater of Sidon (epigrammatist).	100
	Glaucia Prætor, . . . 100				
	Laws of Drusus. His death, . 91	C. Licinius Macer (historian), " 80		Asclepiades (physician).	
	SOCIAL or MARSIC WAR, . 90-88		Sulla on the Euphrates, . . 92		
	L. CORNELIUS SULLA. (138-78)	Valerius Antias (historian), fl. 80-70		Library of Apellicon to Rome.	
	" expels Marius, 88				
	First Civil War, . . 88-86	L. Cornelius Sisenna (hist.), 118-67	Revolt and Siege of Egyptian Thebes, ... 86	Dionysius Thrax (grammarian), fl. 80	
	First Mithridatic War, . 88-84				
	CINNA at Rome, . . 87-84	Q. ROSCIUS (actor), . . d. 62	Sulla, in course of 1st Mithridatic War, takes Athens, . 86	Diotimus the Stoic, . . fl. 80	
	Return of Marius, 87; his death, 86				
	" Sulla, . . . 83	M. TERENTILIUS VARRO, . 116-28	TIGRANES (Armenia), . 95-60		
	Second Civil War. Battle of Colline Gate, . . 82		" at War with Rome, 85-66	Cicero at Athens, . . 79	
	Second Mithridatic War, . 83-81	Hortensius (orator), . . 111-50	Pompey in Africa, . . 81		
	Sulla Dictator. Proscriptions, 81-79				
	CORNELIAN LAWS.				

Political & Military (West)	Literature — 99-55	Eastern Events	Philosophy, Science & Arts
WAR with SERTORIUS, 78-72	LUCRETIUS(?), 99-55	Nicomedes III. leaves BITHYNIA to Rome, 75	POSEIDONIUS (phil.), 86-62
POMPEY, (106-48)	ATTICUS, 109-32	Victories of Lucullus in Asia, 74-66	Ænesidemus (phil.), fl. 80-50
War with Spartacus, 73-71	Laberius (mimes), 107-43	Scythians expelled from India.	Themison (physician), 123-43
Third Mithridatic War, 74-63	CICERO, 106-43	Hyrcanus II. and Aristobulus at War. 74-63	
1st Consulship of Pompey and Crassus, 70	" against Verres, 70	Rome interferes in Palestine (Antipater), 69	Dioscorides (Mosaics).
Pompey defeats the Pirates, 67	LUCULLUS founds Library at Rome, 63	Antiochus Asiaticus dethroned by Pompey.	
Catiline's Conspiracies, 65-63	Metellus (orator) Consul, 60	SYRIA a Roman Province, 65	
CICERO Consul, 63	CATULLUS, 87 (or 84)-54	Pompey subdues PHŒNICIA and takes Jerusalem, 63	Indian Drama flourishes.
M. PORCIUS CATO, (95-46)	P. Ter. Varro (poet), b. 82	JUDÆA tributary to Rome, 63	
Pompey's Great Triumph, 61	Calvus (poet), 82-47	CYPRUS a Roman Province, 57	
Cæsar in Spain, 60	CÆSAR, 100-44	End of the Seleucidæ, 57	
Coalition of Pompey, Cæsar, Crassus, (FIRST TRIUMVIRATE,) 60	SALLUST, 86-34	CONQUEST OF GAUL—	Timagenes the Syrian (hist.)
1st Consulship of Cæsar, 59	Vitruvius (architect), 80-11	Helvetii & Ariovistus defeated, 58	
Cæsar in Gaul, 58-51		The Belgæ and Nervii " 57	
" in Britain, 55-54		Treviri defeated, 54	
2nd Consulship of Pompey and Crassus, 55		Cæsar crosses the Rhine, 55-53	
C. JULIUS CÆSAR (100-44)		VERCINGETORIX & Alesia taken, 52	
MARCUS ANTONIUS, (83-30)		GAUL a Roman Province, 50	

Political & Military (West)	Literature	Eastern Events	Philosophy, Science & Arts
CIVIL WAR, 49-48	C. Asinius Pollio (orator and poet), 76-4	Battle of Carrhæ, in Parthia; Crassus killed, 53	Quintus Sextius (Stoic).
Battle of PHARSALIA, 48	Gallus (poet), 66-26	Cæsar in Pontus conquers Pharnaces, 47	
" Thapsus, 46	First Year of Julian Calendar, 45	Cæsar in Africa, 47	Cratippus (phil.
" Munda, 45	VIRGIL, 70-19	CLEOPATRA, (69-30)	
Assassination of Cæsar, 44	CORNELIUS NEPOS, d. 14	End of the Lagidæ, 43	Library of Pergamus to Alexandria, 40
SECOND TRIUMVIRATE—Lepidus, Antony, Octavianus, 43	Criticism of the best Attic literature at Rome, 30	Antony and Cleopatra on Cydnus, 42	
War with Brutus and Cassius.	MÆCENAS, (b. 74-64), d. 8	HEROD the Great in Judæa, 37-4	
Battle of PHILIPPI, 42	HORACE, 65-8	Agrippa crosses the Rhine, 37	
War of Perusia, 41-40		Antony fails in Parthia, 36	
Lepidus expelled from Triumvirate, 36		" invades Armenia, 34	Pantheon dedicated by Agrippa, 27
War of Octavianus and Antony, 33-31		EGYPT a Roman Province, 30	
Battle of ACTIUM, 31			
Gateway of Janus closed, 29-25			
OCTAVIANUS (AUGUSTUS), (63-A.D.14)			
" Emperor, 27-A.D. 14			

Political & Military (West)	Literature	Eastern Events	Philosophy, Science & Arts
Cantabrian Wars, 25, 19, 13	MESSALA, 64 - A.D. 9	Tiridates seeks Roman Court, 25	DIONYSIUS of Halicarnassus, d. 18
Augustus invested with Tribunicia potestas, 23	TIBULLUS, 54-18	Romans fail in Arabia, 24	
Death of Marcellus, 23	PROPERTIUS, 51-16	Spain finally subdued.	Babrius (poet).
Embassy from India, 20	M.A. Seneca (rhetorician), 60-A.D. 30		
Parthians restore standards, 20		Agrippa in Asia, 17	
German War. Roman defeat under Lollius, 16		Cappadocia Roman, 17	
Tiberius and Drusus defeat the Rhæti and Vindelici, 15	Labeo (jurist), fl. 18	British Commerce with Italy and Gaul.	
Deaths of Agrippa and Lepidus, 12			
Augustus Pontifex Maximus, 12			
Drusus in Germany, 12-9	LIVY, 59-A.D. 17		
Death of Drusus, 9			
Tiberius defeats Germans, 8-6	OVID, 43-A.D. 17		DIODORUS SICULUS (hist.), fl. B.C. 8

Latinity,

VI. FROM A.D. 1 TO A.D. 200. BY PERIODS OF TWENTY YEARS.

A.D.	Rome	A.D.	Other Nations	A.D.	Literature and Art	A.D.
1	Tiberius commands on the Rhine, . . .	4	Judæa a Roman Province under Syria, . . .	6	Ovid banished, . . .	9
	Destruction of Army under Varus, . . .	9	Pannonia, Dalmatia, Rhætia, and Noricum Roman.		PHÆDRUS, . . .	fl. 14
	TIBERIUS CÆSAR, . . .	14-37	Cherusci under ARMINIUS defeat Romans, . . .	9	CELSUS (physician), . . .	17
	Germanicus in Germany, . . .	14-16	Artabanus (Parthia), . . .	14-44	Velleius Paterculus (historian), . . .	B.C. 19-31
	„ in the East, . . .	17	Germanicus in Parthia, . . .	17	STRABO (geographer), . . .	B.C. 66-22
	„ Death, . . .	19	War between Arminius and Marbod, . . .	19		
20	M. ÆLIUS SEJANUS dominant, . . .	20-31	Pontius Pilate in Judæa, . . .	25	Cæsius Bassus (poet), . . .	d. 79
	Prætorian Camp at Rome, . . .	23			PHILO JUDÆUS, . . .	c. B.C. 20- ?
	Tiberius at Capreæ, . . .	26-37			Valerius Maximus (hist.) ?	
	Fall of Sejanus, . . .	31			PETRONIUS ARBITER, . . .	d. 66
	Macro Prefect of Prætorians, . . .	31-37	Crucifixion, . . .	30	Apollonius of Tyana, . . .	b. B.C. 4-
	Agrippina I. banished, 30; died, . . .	33			Philo, Senior Ambassador to Rome, . . .	40
	CALIGULA, . . .	37-41				
	„ Expedition to Gaul, . . .	39				
	„ Assassinated, . . .	41				
40	CLAUDIUS, . . .	41-54	Lycia a Roman province, . . .	43	SENECA, . . .	3-65
	Conquest of Mauretania, . . .	42	Judæa and Samaria directly Roman, . . .	44	LUCAN, . . .	39-65
	Claudius invades Britain, 43. War, . . .	43-51	Thrace „ „ . . .	47	PLINY Major, . . .	23-79
	Execution of Messalina, . . .	48	Frisians subdued, . . .	47	Annæus Cornutus, . . .	fl. 55
	Claudius marries Agrippina II. and adopts Nero,	50	Colonia Agrippina, . . .	50	A. PERSIUS FLACCUS, . . .	34-62
	„ poisoned by „ . . .	54	CARACTACUS Prisoner, . . .	51	Columella (husbandry), . . .	„ 50
	NERO, . . .	54-68	South Britain a Roman province, . . .	51	Pamphila (female historian), . . .	„ 55
	Britannicus poisoned. Parthian and Armenian Wars. Agrippina murdered.	59	Corbulo in Parthia, . . .	56-64		
60	Insurrection in Britain subdued, . . .	61	ST. PAUL at Malta, . . .	61	Silius Italicus (poet), . . .	25-100
	ROME BURNT. Christians persecuted, . . .	64	BOADICEA in Britain, . . .	64	COLOSSEUM built, . . .	70-80
	Conspiracy of Piso. Deaths of Lucan & Seneca, . . .	65	Revolt of the Jews, . . .	65	Papinius Statius (poet), . . .	61-96
	Nero at Olympic Games, 67; Death, . . .	68	Josephus governor of Galilee, . . .	66	Salcius Bassus (poet), . . .	fl. 75
	GALBA, 68; murdered in the Forum, . . .	69	TITUS destroys Jerusalem, . . .	70	Stoics banished by Vespasian.	
	OTHO. VITELLIUS,		Civilis leads Batavian revolt, . . .	70	The Laocoon.	
	Civil War. Otho kills himself. Vitellius killed.		AGRICOLA subdues Britain, . . .	78-85	JOSEPHUS, . . .	37-97
	VESPASIAN, . . .	70-78				
	Batavian, 69-70; British, 61-84; Jewish Wars, 65-70					
	Reform of Treasury.					
	TITUS, . . .	79-81				
	Herculaneum and Pompeii destroyed, . . .	79				
80	DOMITIAN, . . .	81-96	GALGACUS at Mons Grampius, . . .	84	Amphitheatre of Verona.	
	War against the Chatti, . . .	82	Decebal King of Getæ defeats Romans . . .	86-90	Demonax the Cynic, . . .	fl. 80
	Agricola recalled to Rome, . . .	85			Paris (Pantomime) killed, . . .	83
	Unsuccessful Wars with Getæ, Quadi, and Mar-				Valerius Flaccus (poet), . . .	fl. 88

	Domitian killed, ... 96 NERVA, ... 96-98 Relief of Taxes. Distribution of Lands.		QUINTILIAN, ... 42-118 **TACITUS**, ... ? 55-117 PLINY Minor, ... 61-105	
100	**TRAJAN**, ... 98-116 Free Constitution. Judicia Majestatis abolished. Elective Power to Comitia. Free Speech in Senate. Trajan conquers the Daci, ... 101-103, 105 Parthian War, ... 114-116 Trajan takes Ctesiphon and sails down Tigris, 116 3rd Persecution of Christians. HADRIAN, ... 117-138 Surrender of Eastern Conquests, ... 117 4th Persecution of Christians, ... 118	Dacia a Roman province, ... 106 Armenia, Mesopotamia, Syria, Roman provinces, 114 GREATEST EXTENT OF ROMAN EMPIRE. Earthquake at Antioch, ... 115 Picts invade Britain, ... 117 Euphrates boundary of Empire, ... 117	Forum Ulpianum; Column of Trajan, . . . 103 Dion Chrysostom (rhetorician), ... 50-117 PLUTARCH, ... 40-120 Polycarp Bishop of Smyrna, ... 96-166 SUETONIUS, ... 68-	100
120	Visitation of the Provinces, . . . 120, 125, 130 Extension of Commerce throughout the Empire. Quadratus and Aristides at Athens present 1st Apology for the Christians, ... 125	Hadrian's Walls—Newcastle to Carlisle, . . 121 ,, ,, Rhine to Danube, . . . 121 Hadrian rebuilds Jerusalem, ... 130 Revolt of Barcochab in Judæa, ... 132 Dispersion of the Jews, ... 135 Prosperity in Britain under Hadrian.	Statues of Antinous (Hadrian's page). EPICTETUS, ... fl. 117-138 Moles Hadriani (St. Angelo). Edictum Perpetuum of Hadrian, ... 132 Ælian (the rhetorician). Aulus Gellius ("Attic Nights"), ... fl. 143	120
140	**ANTONINUS PIUS**, ... 138-160 Faustina I., ... fl. 138-141 Development of the Civil Law. Establishment of Schools in Provinces. Insurrections in Provinces quelled. Christianity tolerated.	Vallum Antonini in Britain, ... 140 Rome applied to as an Arbiter by various nations.	JUSTIN MARTYR, ... 103-166 Herodes Atticus (antiquarian, &c.), . . 104-180 Fronto (antiquarian), ... fl. 153, d. 166 APPIAN (hist.), ... fl. 147 GALEN, ... 130-200 GAIUS (jurist), ... fl. 160 APPULEIUS, ... 130-174	140
160	**MARCUS AURELIUS**, ... 161-180 L. Verus associated in the Government, . 161-169 Faustina II., ... fl. 145-175 Pestilence and Famines at Rome, . . . 161-166 Wars with Parthians, ... 162-166 Wars with Marcomanni, Quadi, &c., 167-174, 178-180 Greek Philosophers patronised. Rebellion in Syria quelled, ... 175 Christians in Gaul persecuted, ... 177	Verus in Armenia and Syria, ... 161-165 Seleucia demolished, ... 165 Advance of the Goths. Attacks on Dacia.	Celsus (philosopher), ... fl. 160 MARCUS AURELIUS, ... 121-180 LUCIAN, ... 120-200 Irenæus (bishop of Lyons), ... 120-200 Pausanias (geographer), ... fl. 174 P. Ælius Aristides (rhetorician), . . . ,, 170 Hermogenes (rhetorician), ... ,, 170	160
180	COMMODUS, ... 180-192 Perennis Prefect of Prætorians, ... 180-186 Cleander ,, ,, ... 186-189 Commodus as Gladiator. Killed, ... 192 PERTINAX killed, ... 193 DIDIAS JULIANUS buys Empire. Killed, . 193 SEPTIMIUS SEVERUS, ... 194-210 Defeat and death of Niger, ... 194 Battle of Lyons. Death of Albinus, . . . 197 Severus invades Britain, 208-209; dies at York, 211	Byzantium taken by Romans, ... 196 Parthians defeated by Romans, ... 198 End of Arsacidæ, ... } 226 Beginning of Sassanidæ (Persians), ... }	Statue of Aurelius, ... 180 DION CASSIUS (hist.), ... 155- Clement of Alexandria, ... d. 213 Julius Paulus (jurist)? Diogenes Laertius (biographer). Temple of Sun at Baalbec, ... 197 ATHENÆUS, ... fl. 200 HIPPOLYTUS, ... d. 230 TERTULLIAN, ... 160-240 Sextus Empiricus (phil.), ... fl. 225	180
200				200